A ROOKIE READER

OVER-UNDER

By Catherine Matthias

Illustrations by Gene Sharp

Prepared under the direction of Robert Hillerich, Ph.D.

CHILDRENS PRESS ™

CHICAGO

Library of Congress Cataloging in Publication Data

Matthias, Catherine.
  Over-under.

  (Rookie reader)
  Summary: A young boy's frolic in the park illustrates
the meaning of several prepositions. Includes a word
list.
  [1. Parks—Fiction. 2. English language—Prepositions
—Fiction] I. Sharp, Gene, 1923-   ill. II. Title.
III. Series.
PZ7.M43470v 1984   [E]   83-21005
ISBN 0-516-02048-X

Sometimes I'm on.

Sometimes I'm off.

Sometimes I'm in…

…or I'm out.

You might find me over.

You might find me under.

You might find me around…

…or between.

I could be inside.

I could be outside.

I could be above...

...or below.

Sometimes I'm up.

Sometimes I'm down.

Sometimes I'm upside down.

I'm always somewhere…

...doing something.

WORD LIST

above
always
around
be
below
between
could
doing
down
find
I
I'm
in
inside

me
might
off
on
or
out
outside
over
sometimes
something
somewhere
under
up
upside down
you

About the Author

Catherine Matthias grew up in a small town in southern New Jersey. As a child, she loved swimming, bicycling, snow, and small animals. *Wind in the Willows* and *The Little House* were her favorite books.

She started writing her own children's stories while teaching pre-school in Philadelphia. *Over-Under* is her fourth Childrens Press book.

Catherine now lives with her family in the Northwest, where her favorite things are gardening, hiking, fog, windy autumn days, and the ocean.

About the Artist

Gene Sharp has illustrated books, including school books, for a number of publishers. Among the books he has illustrated for Childrens Press are *The Super Snoops and the Missing Sleepers*, *Too Many Balloons*, and several in the "That's a Good Question" series.